ABOUT THE AUTHOR

Juan Cantalejo is a teacher and poet from Liverpool,
England and has roots in Seville, Spain.

A passionate believer in education and in the
transformational power and beauty of art.

He hopes that you enjoy the book and looks forward
to hearing from Prince Neverbudge.

Juan Cantalejo

THE POEMS
OF PRINCE
NEVERBUDGE

AUSTIN MACAULEY PUBLISHERS™

LONDON • CAMBRIDGE • NEW YORK • SHARJAH

A CIP catalogue record for this title is available from the British Library.

ISBN 9781398432673 (Paperback)
ISBN 9781398432680 (ePub e-book)

www.austinmacauley.com

First Published 2022
Austin Macauley Publishers Ltd
1 Canada Square
Canary Wharf
London
E14 5AA

POEMS

His heart broken by love
Taken to the windmills of La Mancha and beyond
Towards the glory of Tresleton
Please may I introduce you to...
The Poems of Prince Neverbudge

A Poem

In you go!
With head or toe
To and fro
Watch it go

There are places to go!
That one must go
If you want to know
It tells you so

Parasol

In sun and shade
By the water it sleeps
Once awoken ...
It sits and stands
Ready to serve
Is there anything more
beautiful than the
umbrella?

2020

Unroll the scroll as far as one can see
There within a place for thee
The torment and treasure of the sea
As the past troubles do fade
The dawn of a new decade
A place and of a time in history
Which discoveries will you see?

Sound

Bite byte bite
Goes the soundbite!
Around and around
Turn up the sound!
Appearing in all colours
Ordered by others
Let the good times roll!
Sell your soul!
We're all in this together!
Hell for leather!
Look out for your neighbour!
Do me a favour!
There's no room in the inn!
Put it in the bin!
Take care of the land!
Chop off both hands!
Keep the waters clean!
No life can be seen!
We're turning the tide!
See you on the other side!

Disease

The virus is coming!
Sisters and brothers
Take cover!
It can be delivered to your door
Not a single word more
Attacking every floor!
When out & about
Button up your mouth
Handkerchief left at home
Wandering into the unknown
Empty pockets?
Please
Remember!
If you sneeze
Greensleeves!
Rain from Spain!

Wash it all away!
Wash it all away!
Wash it all away!

When the sun comes out
Don't forget to shout
Anyone about!

Night or Day (When it comes our way!)

Ready
Steady
Go!
Please allow me
To declare
Here, inside my glowing chamber!
Dressed in my gown
Between, Smile and Frown
That I,
Prince Neverbudge of Tresleton
From this moment
To another
Will give all, unto the air!

And yet

We, You and I, or
They

May lead us down a path
Smack!
May hand you a pill!
Better, still!
Hello Jack and Jill
How cool is the water!
Dear Pinocchio, what happened to your nose?
Let me hand you my hankie
I'm sorry that I missed you
Dear family!
To the Don of all Dons
Don Quijote!
Please accept my most gracious bow

How charming of you
Dear princess!
And now
Yes, now

Would you like another bomb? Or Wannabomb?
They can blow with such aplomb
Bang!
How's that!
Will you miss me when I'm gone?

Into the next life
To be greeted by
Trouble & Strife?

Let the bubble burst
And
Out of the Hearse
Step a group of old friends
"We're off to pick up ...and to be Merry again!"
Yes and thank you Dear friends! I'll join you for
the ride
The everlasting one!

And when that ball hits the net!
Such treasures
How could we forget!

For ...

Why should one shed a tear?
With all this fear!
With foe
No place to go!
Allow me to make this clear!
I believe in each tear!
drop!
But!!!!!!!!!!!!!!!!!!!!!!!!!!!!!!!!!!!!!
When?
How?
Will!
It
Stop!

Passing by

If you can find
hope
And peace of mind
As the days pass by
Why so much change!
As the days pass by
Forever and a day
A day and forever
If you can find
What lies behind
And ahead of tomorrow
Beg, steal or borrow
As the days pass by

Full Speed Ahead Captain!

Come and see!
For a non negotiable sum
What has been done!
"Please, Be patient!"
"Good To Go?"
"Ready?"
"Scissors?"
"Teeth!"

Flash!

"It's....OPEN!"

CRASH BANG WALLOP!
THE MARKET PLACE!
CLICK AND COLLECT!
A LIFE FULL OF DEBT!
FEELS GOOD!
BE THE BEST!

Bulls & Bears
Everywhere!
Top hats & Big cats
Elephants
Disappear into thin air
That's the Circus my friend
And
If you care
To
Rattle a snake

Watch
It

Go!
Up and down
(Send out the clowns)
Then,
And only then
Yes!
It breathes again!

Come on!
Roll that dice
No sacrifice!
Join the game

Open to all
Big and small
Rich and poor
Black and white

That's right!
Fight the Good Fight!

Look!

Way way beyond the child with a kite!

"Where?"

There! There it is!

"Give it a shake!"

The Magic Tree!

What a sight to behold!

Hear, Here!

With the vibration
To here
Clear!
hear
One
Note!
With the vibration
With the vibration
With the vibration
With the vibration
With the vibration
Harmonious creation!

Yearnings and cries
Wallowing and following
Following and wallowing
Higher and lower
Lower and higher
To a sky!

A
Flower, unseen!
Sit amongst them
Hear!

With the vibration
With the vibration
With the vibration
With the vibration
With the vibration
Harmonious creation!
Cheer!
The heart
Let us not part
beat
With the vibration
With the vibration
With the vibration
With the vibration
With the vibration

¡Que aproveche!

¡Anda!
Andaluz
¡Corre!
Catalán
¡Marcha!
Madrileño
¡Fuma!
Flamenco
¡Que bailen los viejos!

Agua
Segovia
Fuego
San José
Toca
Una guitarra
En la Plaza del Rey
¡Viva La Mancha!
¡Los Molinos y Los Vientos!
¡Viva Valencia! ¡Viva
Euskadi! Y ¡Viva El
Pais Vasco!

¡Que vivan todos!

Y
Sueña

Sevilla
Y

A todas las maravillas
Y
¡Que Vivan!
¡La Alhambra y la brisa!

También

Te
Llevaré
De una Sierra Nevada

A
La
Santa Fe

Enjoy!

Walk! / Come on!
Andalusian
Run!
Catalan
March! / Party!
To a citizen of Madrid
Smoke!
Flamenco!
The old folk are dancing!
/ Let the old folk dance!

Water
Segovia
Fire
St Joseph
A guitar
Is playing
In the Kings Square
Long Live La Mancha!
The Windmills and
The Winds!
Long Live Valencia!
Long Live Euskadi!
And Long Live The
Basque Country!

Long Live everyone!

And
Dream!

Seville
And

All of the wonders
And

Long may they Live!

The Alhambra and the
breeze!

Also

Will take you
From a Sierra Nevada
(Snowy Mountain Range)

To
(The)
Santa Fe (The Holy Faith)

Hunger

What's at stake?
When the chips are down
No food around!
A free for all
One last spin!
Banker takes all
To The Laundrette
Try to forget
Change would be good
Climb inside & go for a ride
Then,
Don't!
Hang yourself out to dry
Give it another try!

Tomorrow's Shopping

Let's go to the shops
Along The High Street
The only folk you meet
Live on that street!
Through no fault of their own
We disown!
There will be many more
Living outside, their door!
With new neighbours
Lining the floor
A steep price to pay
For living this way

The Willow Tree

Beneath
The
Willow!
I
Began
To
dream
Of
What
may
have
Been!
Hollow
And
Follow
Ripe!
To
The
Core!
Branches
And
Leaves
Tell
Tales
Of
Birds
and
Of
Other
Trees!
Of
What
may
Be!
Hollow
And
Follow
Ripe!
To
The
Core!
Come
Back
Tomorrow!
I'll
Tell
You
more!
Hollow
And
Follow
Ripe!
To
The
Core!

Palm Sunday

Lord
Rest!
And
Raise!
My
Spirit
To
Be
Within
It
And
Place
In
My
Palms
The
Beauty
Of
Your
Psalms
That
Lay
For
You
As
You
Rode
Into
This
Day
Today

Please, Por favor, Bitte, Snälla du

Let go of the rope
Let it go!
Swing into your life
Rise!
With the sun
Fall!
With a feather
Blossom!
With all of those buds
Where!
The heather does grow
Plunge!
Into the snow
Let the mind flake
Awake!
With
birdsong
And
Make!
A Snowman
Watch it!
Hang on
For all it can
Let it snow!
Let it go!
LET IT GO!

A Slice of Life

Misfortune was met
With
Open arms
Alms!
Grace!
Hand over your fate
With
Open palms
Charms!
Faith!
Fortune was met
A piece of cake
See the,
Cherry on top

Rite

For one has
Right
To do
To be
What is right

Into the darkest night!
Raining meteorites
Silver swoon of the moon

Entered my room!
Into the day
A golden array

For one has
Right
To be
To do
What is right

Domingo

Despertarse
Pasarse por el puente
Pasarse por los muertos
Pasarse por una casa
Pasarse por los leones
Sentirse, Respetarse, Seguir
Entrar por la cancela
Pasarse las flores
En una puerta
Palabras

Domingo – Sunday

Despertarse – To Wake
Pasarse – To Pass/Cross/
Hand out/Stay
Por – By/For/Through/
Over
El – The
Puente – Bridge
Los – The
Muertos – Dead
Una – A/One
Casa – House
Leones – Lions

Sentirse – To Feel
Respetarse – To Respect
Seguir – To Carry on/
Continue/Follow
Entrar – To Enter
La – The
Cancela – Gate
Las – The
Flores – Flowers
En – In/On
Puerta – Door
Palabras - Words

La Vida Smart

Mere mortals open the portal
Welcome to La Vida Smart!
A new world for all
With no end in sight
Get with the program!
What's the matter with you?
Put your thinking cap on
You don't want to be left behind, do you?
Come on!
Be Smart!
You could run for miles
(No more aches nor piles)
Work twenty four seven
Forget all about heaven!
A brand new start!
Life without a heart
Be a part of our machine
Join the winning team
Let someone else push the buttons
Square every root
Pass the time on mute
Simulate simulators
Hang out with aligators
Watch an ice cap melt
Put another on the belt
Be a part of – LV1S – Dream Creation
A La Vida Stream for the Nation
Binge!
Get Wired!
Go on a platinum date!
Go and get your updates!
That's where the real fun begins

The roller of all roller coasters!
(Satan's poacher)
Carpe Diem!
All memory erased
Welcome to The Maze!
In here, you will not find nor feel a thing
Such joy you will bring

Here The Smarts sing
(To the latest algorithm)

Smarts
Around the globe
Do as they are told!

Smarts
Don't have to think
Never on the brink!

Smarts
Are open minded
For us all is decided!

Smarts
Don't have a home
We are free to roam!

Smarts
Never eat
Yet we're the fastest on the beat

Smarts
Don't go to school
We will always rule!

Smarts
Have all the fun
The work is never done!

Smarts
Always party
For our Party!

Party! Party! Party!
We always Party!
Party! Party! Party!
We always Party!

Party! Party! Party!
Party! Party! Party!
Party! Party! Party!
Party! Party! Party!
Party! Party!

"Are you alright?"
"I, I think so, a strange dream"
"Come on!
It's time to party"

Blue

Around, up, down, flowing
Fallen, somewhere
Flowing

The Tide

Nightfall
Days rise
Life, still, full of surprise
Water swims to its tide and opens up
Life's magical tide

Life Force

Passed on songs and dance throughout the years
Words of now and then to our ears
Pictures and Paintings appear
To Have and To Hold and Be near

Light

Round
Beautiful
Triangular
Coloured
Plain
The mirror

Windows

Wander
Into
Nocturnal
Days
Of
Washed
Silence

Mother

In a land where the Mother is true
All may rejoice and play a part too
Give to her as she gives to you

Fall

Purpose met I
One autumn day
In all her splendour
She led the way

Into a cirque
Passing the barn
A yarn
Over the tarn

Where lovers have their say
Down to the village
Thoughts
For another day

A Bird of Tresleton

I need I need I need
Need I
Through its eye
Set sail to the Tresleton quail
Looking down from its branch
Holy Grail Prevail
With a quill and its will
Fly and colour the sky
Through its eye

A Scarecrow's Companion

To liberate you
From this toil
And plant you
In this soil
The perfect foil
There, yes, there
The winds will blow you
You will grow, in the light of the sun
Heavens open and you soar!
The downpour!
Clouds will fill the eyes
Life crawls and life flies, life's born and life dies
Stars twinkle upon the eyes
To liberate you
From it's disguise
Moonlight with starry starry eyes

La Mariposa

Mariposa, mariposa
¡Qué hermosa!
De volar libre
Pintando su cosa
Soñando en una rosa

La Mariposa – A translation

Butterfly, butterfly
So beautiful!
To fly freely
Painting its picture
Dreaming on (inside) a rose

By the sea in Sicily

The trellis of tales
A sea flute!
Mute, the heavenly cast
Father and child with Frisbee in the air
Jokes in a hat, an acrobat
A moment to catch

Palermo

A toast to a ghost
Salute!
A white chair upon the seashore
Palermo, cantare from the 'Domenica' score
Alas! The sky is alight
As one steps into the night

Liverpool

Wack, la, buzz
Whatapool!
Of love, magic and life
As sharp as a knife
Where the blood runs thick
Listen to its fingertips
Away with the Liver Birds!
Into the Mersey and beyond
To a poem, play
And song

Horizon

Forward and Backward were walking along a path
When Backward asked, "What's it like to be
Forward?"
"Don't be so Forward!", replied Forward.
"I'm sorry, for being Backward!"

They arrived at the edge of a cliff
A crowd appeared
"Forward", "Backward"
They cried!

Rumble

Lettuce in the pantry
Fancy
Where turnips watch tomatoes turn red
Peas lie asleep in their bed
Below a tartan shortbread
Aubergine begins to dream
Flies nowhere to be seen
Pink ladies looking for a tangerine
One white onion rolls off a shelf
A bottle cries out!
Shadows and cars pass by
Turkey, will soon say goodbye
For the flour will arise
The Brussels will sprout
The wines will mature
All corks pop out!
The ham that hangs is cured
Yet, you can be sure that as I take off my jacket
(Carefully placed on a packet) and potato to you
In that jar of treacle
Swims a clue
Cheese! Call out the eggs
Rhubarb grumbles
Tins sound and the milk starts to sour
For they know it is the hour
The bean and whistle
Prunes and dates
The plate awaits

To Your Good Health!

Thought of a thought
To think of thoughts
That taught thoughts to think
Drink!
To quench thoughts and think of thoughts
Crossing seas and oceans to dock, port or bay
To be drunk all day

Waterway

Embellish with relish a word on a line
Turquoise tap and porcupine
Figurine and faces out of a hatch
The fishermen catch
Tales of tomorrow unfold in the past
Brushes and brooms sweep the octagonal path
The future appears and begins to laugh
Kaleidoscope and sea a forecast for thee
Lemons upon a velvet tree
Branch misdemeanours mere mystery
Eloquence, elementary
O' The Sea of Galilee

Schoolboy

There was a boy in school
Who didn't want to be a fool
So he wrote a rhyme
That goes, chime! chime! chime!
And asked the teacher "Please can I have more time?"

"Farts"

How many have left us?
And never two are quite the same!
Yet some leave their mark more than others

Rocking Chair

Rocking chair rocking chair what do you see?
A bright little bird upon a white tree
Rocking chair rocking chair what do you hear?
A melody that rings this time of year
Rocking chair rocking chair what will you touch?
That piece of magical dust
Rocking chair rocking chair what do you smell?
An air of freshness and as clear as a bell!
Rocking chair rocking chair what did you say?
Go on, let me rest and enjoy the day

Wish

Children
Hocus pocus and truly focus
Upon the spell of a Diplodocus
A shake of a tail
Hocus pocus and Diplodocus
Inside the nest of a giant Locust
Beaming red eyes
A tale of disguise
Spring!
Akalakaka and Tutatazin
Children
Where have you been?

A Tale and a Snail

I followed, I followed, I followed a tail,
Where I came across a little snail,
Inside its shell, there lay a spell,
Which took me out to sea
Upon the waves and upon the shore,
The fish did jump and the moon did soar,
Ten years later,
The little snail was at my door

Numbers

One six six and twenty two
To name one or two
Twenty four, now there's a door
One hundred and ten a good number then
Seventeen, you may know what I mean?
Three, it may set you free!
One, it's better than none
Minus, minus one.

Letters

Language in a sandwich
Fill the inside and out
Where the sun does arise
Round and round letters abound
Singing aloud
In all shapes and sizes
With their truth and disguises
Delightful appetisers!
Sparkling in crystal
Upon a crescent moon
They dance to her tune
To whom may they not be seen?
The Poet and his dream

Turnaround (Letters may be rotated)

Face to Face
Ear with Ear
Eye eye
Legs walking sky
Sky walking legs
Fried. Lay sizzling the eggs
Holes in the goldfish bowl
A cantata to the unknown

The Poet of Waterloo

The Poet of Waterloo
The Poet of Waterloo
Who took out his pen
And turned everything into glue
Everything turned to glue
The Poet of Waterloo
The sun, the stars, Venus and Mars
The Poet of Waterloo
The Poet of Waterloo
A chu and all was anew!
The Poet of Waterloo

All I See

Anytime I,
Look into a mirror
All I see is the never-never
Never!
Reflection without Question
All I see

Nature's Frame

Whirlwind of fire unravelling desire
The night alone and true
A candle lit for two
Splashes of rain in nature gain
For promise and pain
Long may it reign!

At the Station

Steps into the water
Paths of coincidence
Geometry and golden light
Wonders plight
One more sleepless night

Eve

A place of experiment, where one can see
If one plus one is equal to three
Bring forth new worlds
Echolamonalaterre
With all the fun of the fair

Tomorrow

The day had come to put the pepper with the salt
The bath into the water
Sky into fire
Lower and higher
A night drew
Rainbows and an image
Of
You

Twilight

One
And two
Now with three
One two three four
Five no place to hide
Six with its box of tricks
Seven lies below one at the top

Voices

Dressed in flowers a bicycle spoke
A shake of a spear
The words draw near
On the side of the road ...
A five seven exchange to heaven?
Homes where songs were born
Are a present with the dawn
A muse appears
The first voice you hear

Drama

HeeeEEEEEEEEEEEEEEEEEEEEEEEY
Wooooooooooooooooo
HEEEEEEEY!!!
WOOOOOOOOOOOOO
WOOOOOOOOOOOOOOOOOOOOOOOOOOOOOOO
OOOOOOOOOOOOOO!!!
Nothing!
Bubbles
Nothing
Remember!

My Fair Lady

Madness oh madness
Why does thou despair?
For one solemn care!
Wherever it may be
To flower in thee

Even

Even
Odd
Even with odd
Odd with even
Well
Even

Away, a Way of Knowing

A walk, a walk out walking
A breeze, a breeze a blowing
A tip, a tip a toeing
A roll, a roll a rolling
A fountain, fast and flowing
Out of this world am I going?

The Song

At night
Into my room
The song
In the garden
The song
Down a path
To where a house once stood
There, 3 flew
They know I sing

Alive

Phrases like the melody of time
Blowing in and out of mind
Mine the treasure inside
The hidden hands guide
In echo and surprise
The joy to arise

?

Fill off I see
To You & Me
From a stream
To the sea
A voice telling
Like a tree
"To be or not to be"
Fill off I see

How, Who, What?

How did you know that it was so?
Who told you that it was so?
What made you feel that it was so?
A bow?
A reel?
Reveal

Art

Art,
How I love you!
Art,
How can one live without you?
Art,
Where Art thou?

Dreamers

Pour it out
When in doubt
From a tap
Heavens, that
Make believe
Untie the gift
Leave a tip
When, drunk

The Pool of Tresleton

I live in a pool
There is no fairer school
For fool and foe
I don't know
Wind shapeth the water
The king and his daughter
Surrender I must
For the current is just
A question unto us?
Answer abide the ancient tide with peril and reason
The turn of a season, where fortune does bathe
Golden water rings of the pauper
Falling shell casting spell
Inside
Where a goddess may hide peering from the ocean
A knight on the water
End to slaughter!
Universally tied to the current prescribed
Close your eyes, to the light divine
Tightrope to walk and all that its taught
Collection of thoughts and memories shape
Escape!
To the Garden of Eden
Before, evening fell
Onlookers in the wishing well
Following salt to the shore
A life no more

Supernatural

Words & phrases
Today
May lose
Their way
For example,
Spotless!
Super Clean!
Another example,
Rapid!
Super Quick!
But, not so lean
"I mean,"
(Often heard today)
"It is what it is"
(There is no other way?)
Take your pick
Solid!
Super Strong!
Out of the question!
Super Wrong!
Over the moon! Or on cloud nine!
Super Excited!
Be up the creek! (Without a Paddle)
Super Trouble!
A Barrel of Laughs!
Super Fun!
Ready for the Knacker's yard!
Super's End?

The Author

Words and phrases arise
Fall, collide
Appearing upon the page
Dew and dust
In them we trust
The Poet's touch
Open the book
Which takes a look
At the flight of the dove
Closed with a rose
Its beauty unfolds from its pages
To distant lands and sages
In mother tongues and stables
Read across the ages
Left upon a shelf
Written by someone else

That!

For all that!
That, that & that
With that
& that
How's that?
A rabbit pulled from a hat
Nine lives has the cat
Rainbows
That may well be so
Music, snow and rivers flow
Come!
Surely, it must be that
A stab in the dark
Pounding heart
That's
That!

To a Loved One

Only one wish
To be in
Together apart
To be in
Come now
To a loved one

Run!

Wondering as best I can
A passing life that ran
Brightly, sprightly, innocent
Gladly,
Tender & loving ways
Guide,
A passing life that ran
Through,
Days of an age
With,
No here or after
A passing life that ran
Memories,
Joy, tears & laughter
Alive,
Here and after
A passing life that ran

Bon Voyage!

To think that one is beyond the truth
Youth and old fool
The same school
Let principle be your guide
Hold on tight & enjoy the ride

Excursion

If thought can fly
Then who am I
Not to,
Take a ticket
Fly with it
Aboard an ocean liner
Or in the pocket of a miser
Inside the belly of the beast
Or at the table of a thanksgiving feast
If thought can fly

Love

In love one can
Live
In love one can
Dream
In love one can
Grow
In love one can
Find
In love one can
Die
In love one can

DEDICATION

¡El Padre!

Para, ¡Paré!, Para

¡El Padre!

The Father!
For
Stop!